The Millennial and the Work Place

"How to get ahead in your career and stay ahead"

By
Memory Bengesa

©2017, 2018 by Memory Bengesa
First published by Verengai Publishing House
1/20/2018

ISBN-13:978-0-9995371-0-7

The Millennial and the Work Place
Copyright © 2018 by Memory Bengesa. All rights reserved. Printed in the United States of America. No part of this book may be used or reproduced in any manner whatsoever without the written consent of its author.
www.MemoryBengesa.com

CONTENTS

Dedication xi
Millennial Generation 5
Introduction 5
Preparation: For an Interview 7
Work Place Preparation 15
Attitude 17
Integrity 25
Expectations 31
Tardiness 36
Absenteeism 39
Dependability 46
Critical Thinking 49
Initiation 59
Self-sufficiency 63
Dress Code/Image 67
Professionalism 71
Work Ethic 74
Networking 78
Mentors 81
Get-Ahead and Stay-Ahead 83
Acknowledgements 91

Millennial Generation

Here is what comes to my mind when I think of the Millennial Generation:

- ✓ **M**avericks
- ✓ **I**ndividualistic
- ✓ **L**ovely
- ✓ **L**imitless
- ✓ **E**nergetic
- ✓ **N**eutral
- ✓ **N**onplussed
- ✓ **I**nnovative
- ✓ **A**mbitious
- ✓ **L**eaders

Introduction

Since this is the introduction portion of the book, I am going to literally take the time out to introduce myself. My name is Memory (government and yes! Birth given name); I do not have a middle name (duh! That will take away from the fun).

I have been in Corporate America for about fourteen years in two positions, one that allowed me to be in the field and the other aspect which tied me to the Corporate "stuff" which gave me the opportunity to be on the interviewing, hiring, training and yes unfortunately firing side of the corporate life.

I have been in the position to experience all these measures for the last 14 years. With such a privileged workplace background, I felt that it was time for me to help my fellow Millennials, truth be told; I think we are just misunderstood. I also have been in leadership for about the same time (fourteen years) as well, so I really have gone through it all.

My major reasons for writing this book include:

1. Millennials tend to get a bad reputation in the workplace. (Don't worry, not you of course! Just the other ones!)
2. I am a Millennial.

I am a Millennial who was in a long phase of denial mainly due to the fact that I didn't feel correctly labeled with "majority" of the tags that Millennials have been labeled with.

After I finally accepted my fate of Millennialism, I took a proud hold of my generation and decided to help create workforce ready Millennials. So, here is a big apple cider toast to you my generation cohort! Let us fight this fight together and show what Millennials are made up of!

Preparation: For an Interview

Suffice me to say that in this book, many of my experiences will be templates of growth, and the aim is for them to serve as teachers on several grounds, but I still need to point out that I am not insinuating that Millennials need a lot of help, not at all! Rather, I realize how fortunate I was to have had a mother and father that had been preparing me for the workforce since I was 16 years old and by this reason, I am where I am today.

I totally understand that not everyone has parents that came from corporate backgrounds and or backgrounds that can help you prepare for a corporate job, and I am able to sympathize with such individuals because my heart has literally been fragmented into bits during interview processes where the individual was intellectual but not well dressed, or some had one little thing that they should've known prior to the interview holding them back from the position their hearts desired and which to be truthful, they had the skills to perform. These realizations have made me promise myself that I would guide my generation through this thing called life.

If the baton was passed on to me by my parents, it's only fair for me to pass it on to others too. Picture this: you have exhausted days and months filling out employment forms online and or on your Smartphone (you know how we do), and finally all that arduous work of updating and keeping up with your LinkedIn profile finally pays off. That employer or recruiter emails you and schedules you for an interview. You are super excited, so you post all your excitement on your Facebook page and even snap a "happy" face selfie and you stick it on the "gram" and you make sure all your hashtags are colder than a North Pole winter in the middle of July!

#I finally got an interview, #I am on my way up, #Guess who has an interview, #we started at the bottom now we up here…

Plus, more hashtags for everything and anything that has to do with work and like clockwork, you're maxing out on your likes, cashing in on those likes—like a "like-a-palooza." Your social media is "lit" and all your friends and followers are all of a sudden rooting for your success. Ain't that just super amazing?

So, where does one go from this moment forward? Excitement is running in your blood and out your sweat pores, but when the dust settles you ask, how do I prepare for this moment? Let me take it from here….

After conducting numerous interviews and viewing a considerable number of resumes over the course of my corporate life I can guide you through some "do's" and "don'ts" so that you land that position. I need for you not to feel inadequate at all by any of the things I'd write, understand that while these may be elementary to some, it might actually be the first time someone else would give any thought to it as a potential stumbling block to them landing their dream job. I am only using the common mistakes which I have personally encountered with candidates.

The first thing you want to do is make sure you have clear and concise instructions in terms of the address, the building, the suite number and the name of the person that will be conducting the interview, and if you are unfamiliar with the location, my recommendation would be for candidates to take a "dry run" to the building, and by "dry run," I mean over the weekend and or after work or school that you physically drive to the location of the interview so that you can familiarize yourself with it.

Trust me as tedious as this may seem, all kinds of things can take place on the day of the interview which can cost you that interview, personally I would rather be on the more prepared side than on the less prepared side. If the place is more than thirty minutes plus away, then I highly recommend that on the day of the interview, you leave an hour or fifty minutes earlier than the GPS/Maps time, with this you would have made allowance for weather, traffic and or construction, and if you really want the job, it would be better to be at your location earlier rather than later.

I cannot tell you how many times candidates have turned me off by being late! As a seasoned corporate leader, let me be clear on my stand, as well as on the stand of most others like me: I will not hire a candidate that is late to an interview, my reasoning is that if I do so, I will have to deal with your tardy-behind for the rest of your employment and secondly, when a candidate is late that shows me that this job is not that important to you, and so, the last thing you want to do is waste anyone's time while trying to get a job.If you get there early, stay in your car until it's about ten to fifteen minutes before your interview time, it's advisable to be there early but always remember that you were given an opportunity for a specific reason so respect your interviewers time. I recommend walking into the building ten to fifteen minutes before your interview, as this way, you have enough time to find an elevator, stairs or find the office. I am always on the lookout for a candidate that will be punctual to work, and if this job means anything to a candidate, then they will put forth their effort to be punctual to the interview.

Be sure to research the culture of the organization so that you can dress appropriately, but if you are not sure of the culture, you can always wear "default" interview clothes, i.e. Business casual—you can never go wrong with a pair of black slacks and a dress shirt. Remember, you can always ask the interviewer about what attire to wear. You might not even have to, since nowadays, quite a number of organizations post their interviewing process and requirements on their website. Please make sure that your clothes are well-ironed and or in mint crisp condition, your shoes have to be on point (no holes, not dingy and certainly not dirty), understand that I am addressing matters for those seeking a career in corporate positions. You are the sole focus of the interviewer so, when you show up with dingy and or wrinkly clothes, I must tell you that it sticks out like a sore thumb, I have had to turn down some good candidates strictly because of how they were dressed to the interview (personal appearance).

The type of culture we are in has no room for wrinkles, and so for dingy and unhygienic people frankly speaking; put forward the effort at least for your interview! I have had people come in smelling like an ashtray while trying to get a job at a health care company that doesn't advocate smoking, how do you expect to get employed here? I can never forget this candidate that came for an interview; her scrubs looked like they had just come out from the pillowcase on which she laid her head the night before, I had never seen such wrinkles on a pair of scrubs and I had no idea that scrubs could get that wrinkled.

It was a significant deterrent for me.
It only showed me that if she could dress like that to an interview, then nothing would stop her from dressing like that to work. No-way! That was not going to work because our culture was a professional medical environment. Sure, I understand that not everyone has the money to buy interview friendly clothes but let's be smart about this, you can save a little money, and with as little as $15, you can buy a pair of good pants and a dress shirt from a

Good Will or Salvation Army Thrift store. Don't you dare bring up any excuses, if you can buy outfits for the club and or party for the weekend "turn-up," you sure can save money for work clothes.

With dress code comes body hygiene, I cannot say this enough. Research the culture of the organization for instance if you are going to interview and have a clinical trial at an allergy clinic then your best bet is to lay off the lotions, perfumes and or colognes. Do not be afraid to ask the interviewer and understand that your ignorance of necessary information can cost you that position you desire. There is no such thing as being overly prepared and or asking a lot of questions, I would rather have a candidate ask me questions prior to the interview than to be disappointed when they show up like they are on their way to the club.

For regular interviews, you want to make sure you are well groomed, ensure the hair, facial hair, nails and clothes are up to par. If you are going into a professional environment, then make sure your hair is packed in a neat bun, make sure all facial hair is neatly groomed, ladies! If you desire to work in a professional setting then those ten-inch nails will have to be cut to size, in an era of fake eyelashes and over-the-top hair color, it is imperative that you know and understand your organization's culture! If you are going for an interview to be an Administrative Assistant to a corporate CEO who is not Mark Zuckerberg, then you might want to look like an Assistant and not Nicki Minaj in concert.

#The Millennial and The Work Place   *Memory Bengesa*

True story: I once had a young lady came in for an interview, in a professional setting that caters to a majority geriatric population. This lady came in with the longest eyelashes I had ever seen in my life, her hair was in an interesting rainbow color (no judgment, just observation), her nails were as long as bear claws…if we were an entertainment industry, tattoo shop, hair shop, etc. maybe that could fly, but it certainly wouldn't fly in an organization such as ours! How could she not have known this?

I once had an interviewee came in with a 12-inch sub from subway and a large drink in her hands (true story) she literally walked into the interview room with food in her hands. I was thrown off balance because now I was trying to understand why that food was in her hands to begin with, it made no sense because she drove herself and she could have left it in her car and or maybe bought it while on her way home, it was an interview in which we did not keep candidates for the whole day so I was utterly confused.

What's the truth?

The truth of the matter is that we do not want to hire people to start telling them how to dress, act and behave. We kind of secretly want the candidates already "assembled" parse, and for as long as I have been in management, I can say that dress code and hygiene issues are still by far the most uncomfortable human issues to address, I can tackle any other issues confidently but dress code and hygiene; that is why I am overemphasizing the importance of one's appearance.

Work Place Preparation

By now I am hoping you have an idea of the type of work culture you are working in. If you haven't been hired and are not sure of what their culture entails, I highly recommend doing some internet research about the organization, this one single aspect will help you tremendously; especially for the next sections to come, and as for me I will continually reference a private healthcare industry as that is my background.

Work culture should be a core element of who you are, and if you will fit in with "them" and "them" being your workplace, we live in a time where this decision (choosing a work culture and fitting in with them) is solely up to you. Reflecting on some of our issues as Millennials, I sometimes feel that the reason why most of us are misunderstood is because in our generation, we have a myriad of choices and options.

Think about it, back in the day the average adult had to go to work because they had to take care of their family etc. but nowadays we (Millennials) view the workplace as much more than a paycheck and our way of survival because most of us know our parents got our backs (hashtag spoiled generation), we want it to be an environment where we feel valued and useful, which may be in terms of being intellectually valued, and or having value in our organizations CSR (Corporate Social Responsibility). We want to be a part of something great and something befitting hence most of the people in our generation refuse to settle, instead we job-hop until we find what we want. I almost feel like the other generations think we don't know what we want when in actuality we do.

We just do things Millennially because now more than ever, we are a generation that strongly believes in options and opportunities. After all, most companies have taken away the things that kept one's grandparents and or parents at a job, most companies do not have pension plans, they have skewered 401(k) plans with sucky match-ups and no for-real retirement options (so, why would they think we—the Millennials would want longevity in such companies? Duh! After the ink dries on your application and you are done training, what is the next step for the Millennial?

The workforce! Ok, there is so much to cover under this umbrella so stay tuned as I release fourteen years of experience filled with lots of informative nuggets. I am very excited to unfold each facet so that your workforce experience brings forth rapid growth.

Attitude

Attitude is everything once you are on the job, we all come from diverse backgrounds and even though my parents prepared me for the workforce, I can say they never taught me about work ethic, rather they modeled it before me such that I subconsciously ingrained it. I believe I might have picked up from where they left off. My father was a Corporate Executive, my mother owned her own import and export company in Zimbabwe.

As you can imagine, they were very busy people and there was never a day that went by when I didn't see my parents working, so naturally in my mind I have always had a heavy obligation to my employer because of my background, I already understood how heavily the employer relies on me, which makes me super—committed. I understand that I am being paid to do a particular job. You must understand that your attitude today will determine your success within the organization you belong to.

Since we are on this topic of attitude, I remembered when I hired a new employee, I was so eager to train her, and she seemed like she was excited to be trained, but it almost felt as though once the training started, her motivation significantly dropped. It was actually beginning to seem as though it couldn't be the same person whom I had interviewed that was excited, that was now so filled with complaints.

Within the first 48 hours of training, she was already complaining about the job being overwhelming and she also complained about the job being challenging, mind you; I had not asked her what she was feeling, she volunteered this information to me. I had to keep reassuring her that it'll get better.

Remember that not every trainer and manager is going to be empathizing with you— its either you got it or you don't its cut-and-dry, I understand that freedom of speech is our first amendment right, you also have to understand that there is a time and place for freedom of speech and the workforce is not the time and place, especially when you are being trained. I questioned how long she would last and if we were wasting our time in the back of my mind as I trained her.

Understand that as much as you have to be trained—the trainer is also taking notes of you; most companies have a 90-day probationary period to decide on whether you will be a good fit for them. You will hear me continually say: the best attitude to carry to work is a positive attitude, I more than understand the challenges of learning a new position and I also understand that learning to work at a new position may also be quite overwhelming, but please understand that you cannot express this feeling to your trainer because it does not display a clever work ethic.

For instance, in the lady's case, I immediately began to wonder if we had made the right decision and later discovered that we had not. You need to also remember that the organization is not begging you to work with them, my former boss once told me; "people are replaceable" yes! Honey! That was a wow moment because the reality is he was very right, it's a for-profit organization, and when they hire a candidate, they want someone that can do the job and not waste their payroll money by being unproductive. So, this is my bit of advice for when you go through those challenging moments at work: talk to your family and friends about it so that they can help you get through these moments because the workforce is not a place for complacency, with the exception of that one person with whom you really feel cool with, and can sense a real friendship developing and even then, you still have to watch your back.

From experience, I've seen people turning on people, and it's a nitty-gritty world, you wouldn't believe the volunteered information I have received from people that I thought were friends, my position of leadership has attracted all sorts of people that I knew wanted to get close to me personally and the way most people do it is by snitching on other people. I have known employee information that I didn't want to know from those that were close to these people and vice versa.

The same people that would have been brought to my attention would say stuff about the other person. No one wants to be surrounded by negative complacent people and or attitudes, for the simple reason that they suck all the good energy and positive vibes right out of the room, so make sure you are not a "fun sucker." (Energy Vampire)

You always have to mind your attitude at a new job, there is one type of person on this earth that is a pet peeve of mine (especially in management), and that is the know it all! The same girl I mentioned above in this section who was complaining about her training within the first 48 hours was also a "miss-know-it-all," Believe it or not these types of people crawl underneath my skin like a deer tick attached to the deer's hip.

All I can say to you is that the managers know you're intelligent, so you do not have to prove a thing to them. If they hired you, they know that you're smart and that you are capable of meeting the job description so, please do us managers a favor and stop trying to act like you are smart instead, work on proving yourself to us with your results, the workforce is not a competition for intellect-approval-ratings rather it's an establishment that thrives on results that benefit the organization. At the end of the day, just be your natural self and get those results in, instead of expending your energy on unnecessary stuff.

Don't get me wrong, I appreciate smart people, I admire innovative people, I admire willing people, I admire geniuses, but when you are in training, please "take a chill-pill," as there is a time and place for you to prove your worth and your smartness, challenging the trainer and manager on protocols and or Standards of Operations in which you have never ever been involved in is a bad idea and a bad way to start. I have had some new hires continually challenge me on things they know nothing about (so annoying). Your job is to learn the company, understand your position and master that first; maybe one day you can challenge a peer. I cannot depart the "attitude" section without talking about your overall attitude; there are some corporate life "unwritten-rules." When you are at home and or among your friends, you can treat them however you want to treat them, after all, they are not the ones that are signing your paycheck!

However, when you are at work and the leadership is giving you suggestions and or feedback please don't get an attitude, don't get an attitude with your co-workers even if they get one with you. My philosophy is that attitudes do nothing for you, nothing! Absolutely nothing! Once you are in Corporate America you are in the "big-leagues," you are now working with adults and we all hope they are mature including you and if they are not, try your best to conduct yourself as the adult you are. Ain't nobody got time for attitudes. I should also say that in my experience it's been individuals of all age groups and yes, in their fifties too that have had maturity issues, no pun intended at all.

I had a fifty something year old employee go off on me about a business MEMO which I sent out for a team implementation. This lady literally took a business memorandum that went out to more than five employees as an attack on her and her daughter as if I had nothing better to do.

The wisest step to take would have been to ask me to clarify my memorandum (which I would have been honored to do), but I guess she found it ameliorating to make up (assume) a story in her mind like the MEMO was for herself and her daughter and yes, I am serious (this happened in real-life). Before then, I had never had such an explosion over a memorandum. How do you translate a business document to imply an attack on you as a person? sometimes maturity might not come from those you expect to be mature but that doesn't mean they should change your maturity.

The bottom line is that you as a Millennial like myself, will be enveloped in a work atmosphere with a lot of other people; most times with many of them being older than you, please understand that with the likes of the example above, I have learned that "age-ain't-nothing-but-a-number," always conduct yourself maturely and professionally but also be prepared for the unexpected immaturity from others. I also once had a lady that was way older than my mom work with us who used to literally cry when I approached her to address issues with her work. Of course, that made me feel uncomfortable and awkward, I knew that something was up with her emotions, but this is a fitting example of the shenanigans of the workplace.

I can never forget the time a Nurse Practitioner in her mid to late fifties yelled at me in front of my team (so much respect and maturity—right?) About a policy that had always been in full enforcement (someone didn't get the MEMO?) Since she started working with the team, what was interesting was; this employee she was "defending" always ran late, she never—ever called or texted me to tell me she was running late, so much respect—right? (Note to self: don't be this person!)

So, on this particular day this employee who we will call Marie, was carpooling with the Nurse Practitioner (because we were a mobile company in which we carpooled), this day Marie was scheduled to ride with this Nurse Practitioner, teams policy had always been; we wait five minutes and we leave (contingent upon the person that is running late calls and or texts the manager), after our van had its people and no word from Marie, I put the van in drive (that day we actually left after the five minute grace period—but truth be told we didn't have to wait because she wasn't riding in our van anyways). As I put the van in drive Marie came speeding into the commuter parking lot, jumped in the car with the Nurse Practitioner, once at our destination, the Nurse Practitioner's face was red as a tomato and right—there, in front of my group goes off (like I killed the pope!)

I calmly reminded her; Marie knew the grace period was five minutes, she didn't call or text and besides she was scheduled to ride with you (the Nurse Practitioner), the point being; wouldn't it have been much easier for the Nurse Practitioner to approach me (as the manager) in private and ask about the policy before making an assumption? Anyways! I promise you—cohorts…they say our generation has issues! (We need to reevaluate—that!) They are going to have the Millennial Generation singing R.E.S.P.E.C.T like *Aretha Franklin* when it comes to the work-force!

There also used to be an employee who used her facial expressions to give an attitude, and I was relieved when she quit because a face filled with an attitude is like a burst of negative energy. You need to realize that most good managers out there want to do their job to the best of their ability (we are not ISIS and or the enemy), please do your best to treat your leader like you would want to be treated. No one likes working with difficult and negative energy filled people. Difficult people are like kryptonite except I can't make my mind up on who I would rather work with between difficult people or the "know-it-all," either way they are both a vacuum of energy suckers.

Just because I felt obligated to my employer doesn't mean you have to, for me, I realized all the remarkable things the organization had done for me and I was grateful, but if you feel that where you are today is not worth a commitment and or a sacrifice, then allow yourself true happiness in life and find what fits your personality. Let's face it; most employees' attitudes are a direct reflection of how their organization treats them and what that employee feels about the organization.

Integrity

So many times, while training new hires, I like to always give them a little back story on my employment duration. You should see the various facial expressions elicited by that singular piece of information. I enjoy mentioning the duration because I use it as a way of showing them how possible it is to be in such a giant corporation for a long time. I have attributed the duration of my employment to having integrity as one of my core values.

Integrity is not something that one inherits, neither is it learned in a textbook, rather I feel as though it is something that forms an intrinsic part of one's character, and if you desire to scale the next hurdle, get to the next level or achieve growth in your workplace, you must embrace integrity because that's what can carry you there. I always make mention to all my employees that there is never a situation that cannot be fixed, no matter what it is, there is always a fix. It might not be the quick fix which we often desire within that second or day but perhaps it may be in some months' time or even in a year's time but understand that a solution is always available. You might need to talk to someone else for this solution to surface at times.

Some years ago, I hired a young lady right out of college who I took pride in mentoring as well, she was a stellar employee until she became involved with the wrong type of person, not justifying her character flaw but when this happened, I noticed that her performance started to shift, her focus was different, and after a couple of talks, her situation did not get any better as she continued to see this person. We had entrusted her with a time-sensitive daily drop-off routine for corporate as it was part of her job description.

This particular time the package did not track, and it only took a few days for corporate to figure it out, sooner than later the emails started swarming in like bees to a nest, the issue was the simple fact that this particular package couldn't be tracked according to the tracking number. I asked this young lady if she had made the drop, and she said *yes*, I trusted her as she had been honest all along, so naturally, I responded to corporate, letting them know that she had dropped the package off.

Corporate sent another email with a screenshot that made it clear that the package had not been dropped off, once again I asked her, and she stated that she had dropped the package off. I asked her which shipping location she specifically dropped it off at because this way, we would be able to find out if a driver had been by to pick up the package or not. I was trying to resolve the issue at this moment.

Day five comes about and I get another email from corporate stating that the package had just pinged as being dropped off, now mind you this package should've reached its destination three days ago as it was a very time sensitive package. The snowball to this nightmare started, sooner than later this issue was on the desks of top-level executives in corporate and there was nothing I could do at that time but to confront her again.

I had to ask her one last time because by now, this issue was so deep in corporate and ironically enough the company had been contemplating on switching shipping services, my boss called me to see if I could join a conference call about this issue as it would serve as a great example on why we ought to switch our corporate shipping account to a more efficient carrier.

Intuitively I wanted to ask her one last time because I did not want to be the one to cause our company to make an official switch over something that was not accurate, and this time, I approached her in privacy to clarify issues one last time because it was not making any sense. I told her what was getting ready to happen and that corporate was going to investigate this incident, which they were currently doing.

After I was done talking to her, she was in silence as though in deep contemplation and then the next thing I saw was tears streaming down her cheeks, with a confession on her lips! She mentioned that she gave the package to her boyfriend to drop off, she asked him if he had dropped it off when corporate started looking for the package and she said he told her he had dropped it off and she believed him. She found the package in her car days later in the trunk, panicked and dropped it off immediately.

"There is never a situation that cannot be fixed, no matter what it is there is always a fix, it might not be within that second and or day but perhaps it may be in some months or a year but understand that a solution is always available, sometimes it takes for you to talk to someone else to help you bring a solution to the surface."

I repeat the above paragraph so that you can really understand the severe consequences of some cases of negligence. Once she told me the truth, I had to immediately contact my boss to let him know because there was no way I was going to sit in a conference call over something we did.

Your manager's job is not to cover any of your mistakes. After I spoke to my boss, I had to terminate this young lady's employment (yes, she was fired) that day. I have never taken pride in firing employees or in serving disciplinary actions but it's very unfortunate when there are so many actions that could've been taken to prevent such consequences.

After I asked her the first time, all she had to tell me was that she gave the package to her boyfriend to drop off, which was a big no-no because it is health information; but at least we would have had a clear understanding of the situation. In that situation, she would have most likely received a verbal warning. Had she told me the truth from the start, I could have most likely helped her along the way. It was in fact, the lack of integrity that cost this bright lady her job.

She did not lose her job because of a "package" but rather what that package represented. This very package had information that backlogged the results process of our participants which affected a lot more departments and the participants. You need to understand that one "little" mistake can enlarge and give rise to horrible consequences.

I have seen a lot of employees lose their jobs over integrity issues, managers have lost their jobs because they used the corporate credit cards for personal shopping (You would think they would at least know that everything can be tracked). Not only do they lose their jobs, but they also end up with a theft charge. All those years of experience have gone down the drain. Do you want to survive like a champ? Then you need to armor yourself with integrity, no matter what you think; remember that there is always a solution, be the first to talk to your manager about it.

As a matter of fact, I have had employees create huge errors, the types that would have made them candidates for termination but because they had the integrity to address the issue quickly and appropriately, they got pardoned because together we were able to resolve the crisis. In this young lady's situation, had she told me the truth the minute she found the package in her trunk, I could've made some calls and the whole situation could've been diffused, emails (communication) would have reached the appropriate departments and she would have still had a job.

If you ever find yourself in a pickle and are completely nervous and or scared, be sure to get the right help. I have also had some employees try to fix their "boo-boo's" before coming to me and that only made their situation worse.

I recently had a girl use one of our field laptops to connect to a WIFI location after all her training and verbal warnings not to, she still did it. After this specific work day, she could not upload patient images and records, and after I stared at her computer and made sure all connections were sufficient, I noticed that she was connected to a local WIFI, so I disconnected the WIFI and connected to our secured in built WIFI and then to our security platform. I asked her why she was connected to a local area WIFI and she stated that she was having trouble connecting to our network which is secure by the way, so she went ahead by her own decision and connected to the local area WIFI.

I reiterated to her again never to do that because she was jeopardizing patient information. Her one "little" mistake could've cost our company millions of dollars if patient information leaked out. I admire people that are sharp and take the initiative but please don't take the initiative when it comes to matters you know nothing about. I would rather you cross-reference and still have a job at the end of the day. As a manager that is concerned about an employee's development, I think it is better to approach your leadership team so that they can use their combined expertise to assist you and then next time you are in the same conundrum, you will know exactly what to do.

Expectations

It is inevitable for your workplace not to have a set of expectations for you, I always suggest that you make it your business to know them and understand them, since each industry or organization is different. However, I will talk about what should be "common knowledge" expectations in the next paragraphs to come.

Before we dive into the meat and potatoes (Midwest style) or the kale salad and grilled chicken (West coast style), let me start off by mentioning the importance of establishing personal expectations for yourself prior to starting your new "job."

Your personal expectations can solely be centered on your growth within your new organization, understand that for the most part, big organizations want to encourage or boost internal promotions before they can even think of recruiting outside so, yes! Not only are you an employee but a potential asset to the growth of that organization so, therefore it's important for you to set aside a couple of expectations for yourself as it aligns with your new work-place. Setting personal expectations for yourself can help keep you focused and grounded in your position.

If no one within your organization has mentioned any expectations, then I suggest you read your employee handbook from cover to cover and understand what the organization expects from you. If there is no employee handbook, perhaps you can find answers on the organization's website or you could reach out to the Human Resources department.

Once you figure out what the organization expects from you as their employee, you can set expectations for your growth and in case you are wondering why I am not saying goals, I feel as though goals are very personal in terms of things you do for yourself outside of work i.e. losing weight, joining a cake baking class etc. and we all know the track record of accomplishing goals.

Also, some people don't like feeling pressurized over their goals. e.g. if you set a goal to be the CEO in five years, what if five years comes and goes and you haven't even shifted from your current position? That could be very frustrating, whereas an expectation could be to fully master so-and-so program after two months or to work on two different projects in thirty days seems to be more realistic and rewarding. I am not against goals, I utilize goals for my personal life endeavors out of work, and as for work, I have always utilized expectations because there's no room for options. For example, I expected new employees to be trained and signed off within three weeks no buts because it's an expectation.

#*The Millennial and The Work Place*   *Memory Bengesa*

In the workplace, there is a lot of weight placed on expectations, the company hires you and expects you to fulfill your job description (above and beyond would be a plus), a company doesn't hire you and have goals for you to hope that you meet them, rather they figured that those expectations are why they are paying you, so expectations are non-negotiable.

Establishing workplace expectations earlier on in your career will help you create a routine that will eventually be driven by success. When I started with our company I was an Assistant Manager, I read the handbook and started learning more about the company and my position, and when I figured out my job description, I never became comfortable because I expected myself to excel within the company and nothing short of that would be acceptable. After ten months of being on the job, I started to learn other things that were not a part of my job description (I have always been an inquisitive person).

I wanted to know what managers do, and I wanted to learn all aspects of the business so much so that after sixteen months, I was able to fit in as regards to other responsibilities that were not initially my job description. This became an added advantage because I was able to help the company on a national level.

Three years after being hired, I landed a promotion and not because it was there but because I was ready prior to my promotion I had immersed myself in the knowledge of the company and the different job descriptions. The point I'm trying to make here is that if you expect to excel and climb the rungs of Corporate America, then I suggest you roll your sleeves up and get involved everywhere you can get involved which means going past your job description. If you desire progression in your employment status, then I suggest you draft a personal expectations list, one that you can possibly keep at your desk or as a screen saver, so you have a continual reminder. (Preparation and great planning will always make for a great opportunity).

The benefit of understanding your job expectations will also help you align with why you have been hired. I remembered when I got a new hire who struggled somewhat with her job description, she had received her full three weeks training and materials, she had passed all the written tests but when it came to grasping the concept of her job description as it came to multitasking, she seemed to struggle, intuitively that would be an area I would have been working with her so she can gain her muscle.

I remember having a one on one call with my boss who stated that this new hire had emailed him telling him that she would be suitable for a certain position, one she wasn't even trained and or signed off in, not only did she go over my head but she reached out to my boss who had nothing to do with the specific staffing on my team (this story will be unraveled in chapters to come) but I mention it to say, had she read all her materials and read the handbook front to back she would have understood the chain of command and not only that but she wasn't ready developmentally to shift anywhere because she was struggling with what I initially hired her for.

My Dear Millennials, I feel you (hey! I am one too) but doing things out of order in a corporation can jeopardize your growth steps. Please realize the importance of understanding your job description and expectation per your organization. I know most of you are as zealous, if not more zealous than I am, I understand. You are coming out of school, and you have a thing or two to prove to the older generation; I get it, but there is also a process, do your work. Put in your groundwork too (thoroughly understand your job description and fulfill all those expectations), the older generation are where they are in Corporate America because at one point and time they put in their time too.

The chances of instant success are highly unlikely; most people start from the ground up and build up to where they are. Oprah Winfrey didn't just come from University and land her own show and or network, instead, she had to do some work first which comprised of her being on the news in her local town, getting the experience, exposure and comfort, she would need to step into her true authentic self. It tickles me when new graduates come out of school and the ambition is on hundred, its great but be realistically unless your dad is Warren Buffett and you have connections; chances are you will be entering the workforce like most people (at the bottom) and your endeavor should be to hang in there and learn everything well so you can get to where you are going or where you need to go.

Tardiness

This is a biggie! (I sigh). My heart has been ripped into shreds by the number of talented employees that I have had to part ways with because of tardiness, this is a big part of our organization because of the nature of the business. Even though it is in our handbook, you would think people would know better by reading it and understanding the seriousness of this flaw.

As a manager, I am not big on excuses, as a matter of fact; I don't like excuses. Among many other examples, there was a talented young lady right out of school who started working with our organization, this girl had a problem with tardiness. I gave her enough verbal warnings, but her habit continued. When talking fails I resort to documentation, and one would think if you are getting written up, you will make it your sole business to make it work on time, right? Wrong! She continued to come late.

What's crazy about this one particular young lady was the fact that she always ran late to work yet would have a breakfast bag from a fast food restaurant. This young lady, a mother of young twin babies met her termination on her fourth disciplinary action and then she had the nerve to have an attitude but it was her actions that led to her demise. I do not know about the organization you desire to work for and with but do yourself a favor and understand all the policies in the handbook.

My stand on this is that if it takes you thirty minutes to make it work, you might want to leave your home an hour early, as that gives you enough time to allow for any mishaps on the way to work. If you know you are going to be late, in this cell phone age, make it a point to call someone at the job (most likely your boss) and let them know immediately.

Also, when you show up be apologetic. I had a new girl who ran late and was one more grace from a disciplinary action, she didn't call but rather would stroll in late to work with a Starbucks drink in her hand (excuse me?) See, my thing was okay; she is a few minutes late, but can you at least acknowledge through an apology since you didn't call? Not acknowledging her tardiness made me know that she was aware of the fact that she was late and merely strolling over to her work area did not bring favor to her tardiness. I am always willing to give new hires a few chances, but it can never become a regular habit, if you seek advancement and or a raise in some organizations, this can possibly count against your character.

The workplace especially Corporate America is not like that little first job you had out of high school where you could say about anything to get yourself out of trouble. Corporate America comes with polices and tons of rules, the rumor is we are not a responsible generation, let's prove them wrong. Things happen, perhaps you have given yourself more than thirty minutes in allotted time and for some reason, that accident on the highway has not been cleared yet and it seems as though you are going to be late to work, please remember to communicate.

 Tardiness can be eliminated if you give yourself an allowance of more than the time required to get to work and whenever you're caught in an unpredictable delay, communicate well in advance even if it means leaving a voicemail. I am highly impressed by employees that show up for work super early, it says something about their character.

Absenteeism

Confessions of a manager: staffing is a big responsibility for most managers; part of my job is to make sure that I have the right staff at any given point in time to handle the workload so that the company can ultimately meet its revenue goals. I understand that unforeseen things happen because that is a part and parcel of life and because of that accountability goes a long way (once again it all depends on what your career goals are), if you aspire to grow in that company or even become CEO at one point in time, I suggest that when those unforeseen events happen, make sure to hold yourself accountable for providing the right documents to excuse your absence.

I also need to reiterate that when you turn in your documents to excuse your absence, some companies may choose to investigate. Years ago, I had a lady understand that our process was absenteeism by documentation. This lady said she was sick, and she missed the entire day of work only to call me at around 6pm to tell me that she was in the emergency room, I told her okay, just don't forget the note when you come to work.

She showed up to work the next day with a note, of course, I was already suspicious of her note, something did not look right (miss-slick) was not so slick, the note she gave me didn't have a time, so it led me to question the time of check-in, so I followed up with a call to the hospital and asked what time she checked in and sure enough, the time on record was 4:00pm. The problem here was that on this day, the work schedule was from 9:00am to 2:00pm, so she went and "checked" herself in at 4pm, which did not explain where she was during the work hours hence she lost her job. Remember: integrity is one of the core values and lying on absenteeism and producing false documents was reason enough to dismiss her from her employment.

    I seriously can write multiple volumes on employees. I had another young lady think she could outwit the absenteeism by documentation policy, so she ended up not calling her employer that morning when we expected her to come to work, instead she texted an employee who was working with us that day and told her to tell me that she was in the hospital. Of course, this is not contacting the employer still, so when I finally got a hold of her she stated that she couldn't text and or call.

    I asked her if she was brought into the Emergency Room incapacitated or comatose, she replied that she wasn't and once again, her employment was not long-lived. I can seriously write a book on employees who fire themselves, we hired a young lady, a mother of three who was planning her wedding as well (great for her). We actually hired her as an employee referral, three weeks later, the first Friday she received her first paycheck (I don't know maybe it was just coincidental, but I am just saying—its mere observation on my end) so, on this particular Friday she decided not to show up for work, she did not call me nor text, nothing!

Her friend who had referred her told me that she wouldn't be coming but her friend was not the manager! The handbook clearly states that an employee is supposed to call and talk to the manager, and her failure to do so caused her status to fall under job abandonment. Hence, her career was very short lived.

Remember that earlier I sternly mentioned that there is no work situation that cannot meet a resolution no matter what it is, the resolution might not be now, tomorrow or the next day, but every situation can be fixed, all she had to do was to call. There are rules, policies and or Standards of Procedures for this thing we call the "work-place" so please adhere as instructed in the writings of your organization's documentation.

If you value your employment, then maintain integrity at all times. For the longest time, it bothered me when I had to fire people and or issue a disciplinary actions (write-up), I just hated the feeling because I felt sorry for people, as some of these people had families and children to take care of.

The worst memory I have of firing someone was a young girl that couldn't absolutely grasp the concept, she was a liability more so than an asset, on that very day that I had to do it, she mentioned that she had just been evicted from her apartment and her grandmother had just had a stroke and was in the hospital. This was very sad, believe me; managers have hearts too but as Corporate America goes, it's strictly business not personal, we had exhausted all efforts trying to help her but she just couldn't get it. We had done all we could do that was in writing to do and the next step was to cut all ties.

That seemed to be the hardest day of my life until I talked to my younger sister who also happened to be in leadership, she said something that was profound, that helped me isolate my feelings from my job when it came to firing or granting disciplinary actions to employees. She made a simple statement that I did not fire her, I paused and was in a state of confusion because I had just done it, I asked her what she meant by that and she said Managers do not fire people or write people up—people are the ones that fire themselves and write themselves up through their behavior, we (the managers) are just filling out the paperwork. Huh! Wow! *Sissy-Pooh-bear* was absolutely correct. (Don't worry she knows her pet-name), even though she's well in her thirties, she's still my *pooh-bear*!) I realized that I didn't ask the first girl to falsify her note, it was in fact, her lack of integrity that cost her job, I didn't ask the other girl to text a co-worker in her absence but rather, her lack of integrity also cost her job, I didn't ask the new hire not to call me on Payday Friday rather, her lack of integrity cost her job and lastly, I didn't ask the girl that couldn't fulfill her job responsibilities not to be invested and not to dial into her job description instead her unwillingness to learn cost her job.

You see, Ladies and Gentlemen, it is when an individual's personal behavior goes against the organization that they get into a position where they are released or documented, driving without insurance is against the law and everyone with a driver's license has to know this because this is part of the driving test, so, hypothetically speaking, if one gets pulled over and gets heavy fines and or consequences for not having insurance, does that become the officer's fault or problem? No, it's apparently the driver's problem.

Maintain integrity and you won't find yourself on the other side of the tracks. It's really that simple. When I was in school back in the day, absenteeism was held against my grades as well, and in Corporate America, it can be held against your climb to the top. No one will ever be assigned to the next level's responsibilities if they have a track record of unexplainable absenteeism, and so, if climbing the rungs of the Corporate Ladder is one of your desires then understand that everything you do for that organization is under observation.

Those that make it to the top possess specific qualities that the organization knows will take their company to greater heights.

I have employees give me copies of traffic tickets/court summons. I have had an employee in the hospital with her thirteen-year-old daughter and I have had her give me supporting documents, I have been handed tow papers, police statements. I know—right! But there is nothing such as being too accountable, matter of fact I appreciate an employee that is accountable because this builds trust.

What some people don't understand is that: in some work places when an employee wants to transfer or apply for a promotion the feedback typically comes from that department manager, so, don't burn any bridges before crossing over. I had an excellent employee move from a neighboring state, she was sharp. She was signed off within a week and half whereas most people utilize the full three weeks, she was polite, she knew her job description, as soon as she had moved to our state she realized she had to move back, the reason she was moving back to her home state was because she realized that she needed to relocate closer to her family since she had a young family.

She turned in a transfer for the state she came from because there was an open position, so, one would think that's "easy–peasy" right? No! The problem was, as much as she had excelled, she was "just" an employee, she came to work and didn't care to go above and beyond even at times gesturing "I just work here" and secondly, she was known for absenteeism, what she didn't understand like some other people is that your department manager will be the first person to answer questions about your transfers, promotions, employee statuses and everything pertaining to your employment.

It was a sad day, but I have an intense sense of moral integrity meaning I will never lie on anyone's behalf. Therefore, when the director for that region enquired about her, I told her everything about the employee and the unaccountable absenteeism, that plus the fact that the director cross checked some of the questions they had talked about, and this employee had lied to her. Remember I said she didn't go above and beyond, so she told the director all the other things she did which were lies and there goes her integrity! Of course, I clarified that she had lied to the director. Needless to say she never got the transfer.

If you plan on growing within your organization and even plan on opening your own business, work on those things that can hinder your current progress, hold yourself accountable to your current position, and be responsible by being transparent about your absenteeism.

Dependability

Dependability is directly related to tardiness and absenteeism. When your organization hires you, the chances are that they expect you to be at work on your scheduled days as they will rely on your productivity; if they didn't need you, they would not have hired you.

If you truly desire to grow within your career or you desire a promotion or a raise, the best life practice you can have from the start when you are hired is to be a dependable employee. I personally appreciate dependable employees, I know that I don't ever have to worry about them frivolously calling off and leaving us hanging, and to add to that, I always feel compelled to fight ten times more for those employees that are by my side through thick and thin without incident.

Around 2008 and 2009 when the country started experiencing an economic crisis, our company had to downsize, it was a terrible period for a lot of employees in the organization because the company was closing a lot of team, by then we had managed to expand across the borders on an international scale, we had also managed to double the number of teams across the nation.

Before this time business was doing well and of course, no one could have ever seen it coming.

That day came for me, it was after 5pm in the fall, I was driving home from work when my cell phone rang, I looked at the phone and noticed an area code I was reluctant to answer, I pulled over because I worked in the Midwest and the corporate office was in another state with a different area code which I recognized, after I pulled my car over I answered my phone.

"Hello." I said.

"Mem." The voice on the other end exclaimed.

"Kevin." I reluctantly said. Kevin was my boss at that time and for the longest time that we worked together, I knew that he never called me after 5pm my time, I turned down my radio and automatically became nervous because I knew this was it. I had known of the teams being closed permanently so surely this was the call, my heartbeat was racing fast, my palms became sweaty, my eyes started to get a little watery as in preparation for the news.

Kevin asked me if I was driving and I mentioned that I had pulled over, he said that was good, I could tell that he was stalling and finally he mentioned he had some unwelcome news. I couldn't reply because I was dumbfounded, then he said the sad news was that my team was shutting down. Immediately I gasped; trying to cry softly so as not to get caught crying, but within me, it felt as if my entire world was crashing. I had just had my dream house built from the ground up two years earlier and now this?

Without hesitation, he continued talking and said there was also good news. *What? Wait? There is good news?* I silently thought. He said the good news was that he had room for me on the other team, along with one other employee, saying that the company would be remised to lose me as an employee. I quickly gathered myself as the light at the end of the tunnel had just shown up at the start of the tunnel. He asked me if I had an employee in mind and of course I did! The one that had never called off, the one that was accountable, and the one that went above and beyond, the one that was friendly and yet was innovative and very positive.

Don't get me wrong, it was hard knowing that I couldn't take everyone but the one I chose to go with me was a top-performer, I didn't have to even think hard and long.

What a sentimental story and what does that have to do with dependability? I am glad you asked. It has everything to do with dependability, when I initially hired her (the person I chose) she never once expressed to me her goals or desire to climb the rungs of Corporate America, rather she was actually hired for a position at that time that was known for not crossing over into leadership but because she chose to develop herself, and was a stellar top-performing employee with zero absenteeism, never being late, as a matter of fact, she was always early and was the last one to leave alongside with me, it was easy for me to choose her above others.

Critical Thinking

What comes to your mind when you hear "critical thinking?" I know what should come to mind but here's the deal. I totally get it! Colleges for the most part do not have practical sessions on critical thinking, I know some colleges offer critical thinking classes but over the years there's been a lot of debate whether such classes were successful or not.

I feel as though critical thinking should be a part of people, like an intrinsic part of their work ethic. From my work experience, I have noticed that you cannot teach "common knowledge or common sense stuff" you have to come with it, Corporate America is nitty-gritty, you would not believe how much they would rather have a new employee come to work "already assembled" rather than to start "assembling" when the employee starts work (assembled meaning an analogy of an employee coming to work already knowing how to work than starting from scratch).

The reality in today's world is that training costs companies' money, and because companies do not like to waste money, most times they figure out that if they hire people that "they think are experienced," it can cut down on training costs, etc. This is why most new grads have a challenging time finding a place in their dream careers. I am not insinuating that you will never land that ultimate gig (Never that!), I am just stating a fact from my observation of job placements.

Nowadays most employers will state in an employment search that they want a candidate that can work independently and independently doesn't just refer to being able to fulfill the job description on your own, it also falls into the Critical Thinking realm, you are able to fulfill the job description, but you are also able to think independently, they want to know that once they hire you and train you, your every move doesn't depend on others.

I had a girl who we hired and trained, mind you in my line of work I wasn't just sitting in an office, I was also out in the field with the staff working, I had the role of manager and I was an active Clinician, during the whole period that I had worked in this dual position, I had never experienced the ways of this girl. Mind you we hired her for a Customer Care position which is pretty much a front desk position and the go to position for all the participant's questions.

After we trained her, I literally had about three or four people at separate times sent back to my area of work to ask me questions, and they stated that the girl at the front desk told them to come and talk to the manager. Not In a million years had this ever happened. She was supposed to diffuse and resolve any issues and not pawn people off to my area as I was working, so, I had to have the awkward conversation with her, I insisted that it was her job and never to send anyone back to me, if there was a question she did not understand, she could personally come and ask me but she couldn't pawn off participants to me.

I cannot vacate this subject and not tell you my ultimate story-of-all-stories. Earlier I talked about how most leadership does not care for the "know-it-alls." I had a lady who joined our team at the tail end of her education, she had been finding herself in life (which is cool) she was in her early 50's, she was the type of candidate that knew it all but was really not even intellectually present (that's the nice version), she was the type to come and ask you a very logical question and when you responded she would tell you that she knew that already.

This behavior had caused most people on the team to be reluctant in helping her but guess who couldn't withdraw? Me, of course because I am in leadership so after learning from people like her, I knew that all I could do is counter her with questions on top of her questions because if I gave her an answer she would know it already, let me tell you that she was not the "know-it-all-have-it-all," those are less annoying because those people tend to be smart and tend to actually know a thing or two, she was not really an intelligent "know-it-all" rather a "wanna-be-know-it-all," so hence; she acted like she knew it but she had no idea!

True story: I am at work, minding my business, Miss-wanna-know-it-all strolls over to me, mind you there is a test she has to accomplish that requires a race category (not ethnicity) the form only has Caucasian, African-American, Asian, Hispanic and Other, that's it! She comes over, has a gentleman at her station whose first and last name is authentic Italian, I had spoken to the guy and loved his accent, he had a thick East coast accent, I had joked with him on how he reminded me of the *Godfather,* he said he got that a lot, so, this Clinician walks over and asks me what category race to mark? No, it wasn't her first day at work.

I of course give her a cold stare because she can't be serious, so I ask, are you serious? She said well ya! He is Italian, and I don't want to mark the wrong category. There are some things I just can't control in life, one of them is my facial expressions and the other is the stuff that comes out of my mouth, so I burst into laughter and asked her, is Italy not in Europe? (I didn't know with all this Brexit stuff if Italy decided to relocate to Africa or something. Maybe I didn't get the MEMO) then she wanted to act like she didn't hear me, she said excuse me? I repeated myself again, is Italy not in Europe? Then she looked at me dumbfounded, I told her Italy is in Europe, therefore technically folks with ancestors and lineage from Europe are considered Caucasian.

I could've given her the whole story of the Caucasus Mountains to throw her off and by the way she is of Caucasian decent and I folks am an African. I just mention that to say shouldn't she know this out of all her wanna-be-smartness? Don't act like you know-it-all when there are things you don't know because at the end we always see right through you. I will be the first to admit I don't know it all! I purposely try to learn something new every day whether its at work or out of work, the universe has so many lessons.

That was not a question you literally go on the look for a supervisor for, she had been doing that same test for some time, it was not her first rodeo, if critical thinking is not innately in you, I suggest you pick up the only thing we really know how to maneuver which is our smart phones, I don't get paid to think logically for anyone, the workforce is B.Y.O.B (Bring Your Own Brains) and functioning brains that is.

What is critical thinking in my books anyways? After 14 years of management I can honestly say that I appreciate people that come in with a "willing" attitude, unlike some, I like to hire a diversity of new grads and those that have experience only because I feel that everyone needs a starting place and those that are seasoned can impart wisdom to those that are just coming in.

Critical thinking is not that complicated, I look at the ability to take the initiative, willingness to learn, willingness to follow instructions, act upon instruction, being teachable. Being able to take initiative goes a very long way, understand that once you get hired, your employer will focus on you for the next 90 days (some less some more), they will gauge your performance, assessing if you are progressing or regressing, that is also a time for most companies to decide if that position is a good fit for you, so make it your best practice to learn and know your job.

Oh-yes-honey! All eyes on you for those first 90 days, what does this mean? I always tell new hires this: "do me a favor, help me by taking notes!" unless it's not your first rodeo then you are excused, for the rest of the "come-straight-out-of-college-and-I-am-ready-to-work" crew this is for you, if it is your first rodeo then prepare accordingly, invest in a little notepad and take notes that you can remember— remember you most likely have 90 days to make it or break it, taking notes means you have a reference point.

I am one person who doesn't like to repeat myself, I personally like to hand new hires a little informational packet with a "to-do" list which I think will help new people know exactly what they need to accomplish by the end of the day, I get it, not everyone is a "list check off" type of person, you are the only one that knows how you retain information so however you retain information, make it your best bet to learn.

Secondly, taking notes is very impressive to the trainer because it shows them that you are thirsty to learn from their fountain of knowledge, however do not take empty notes, I cannot tell you how many people have taken notes and two months later would come to ask a question about the same thing that they took notes on. Corporate America has no patience, seriously, most companies would rather hire people with experience because they feel like they do not have to do so much in training and spend so much money on training, so you better be quick on your toes otherwise she (Corporate America) will chew you up and spit you back into the unemployment ally quicker than you can say: *super-cali-fragil-istic-expi-ali-docious* (sorry, had a Mary Poppins moment). Thirdly, pay as much attention to detail as you can during your training, take your training seriously as well, be sure to ask all the relevant questions and do not try to act like you know it all especially if you have never worked for that company, look around you, see what others are doing that have the same job description as yours and take some mental notes and visual tips. When in Rome do as the Romans.

With that saying, be very observant to all the right tendencies, it tickles me when people start working and they do something that clearly they hadn't observed, I had a new hire pick up her cell phone! Yes! During work, she knew the cellphone policy and yet went ahead, what baffled me is why would you do that? Now I have to tell you again what you should know, and I know that she hadn't seen any other employee on their phone.

I always admire people that are solution oriented versus problem-oriented, those candidates that seek solutions always hold a special place in my heart because they make my job easier, and which manager or boss wouldn't like that? Such people let me know that they want to move forward with something positive, those folks that tend to be problem-oriented always seem to be the negative ones: "the copier is broken...I have a thousand sheets to print, what am I going to do? There goes my day!" Versus "the copier is broken, let me call the 800 number and try and get someone to help me troubleshoot this so I can finish my project."

Some aspects of Critical thinking go as far as prioritizing the important factors of the organization, every for-profit organization is typically driven by numbers, whether you know this or not, the end goal is top numbers across the board, higher revenues, fewer wastes, higher production, high customer satisfaction scores and or reviews and each organization has its specific numbers and goals for those departments.

Recently I faced something I had not faced in 14 years of my employment history, I had three employees hired that where underperforming, I always make it a point for all individuals involved on the team to understand what is required of them by the organization especially number wise. I am very competitive and this particular year the numbers where tanking, I thought they were going to have to admit me to the asylum because the good Lord knows I was trying everything but when you have folks who don't have passion for what they do; that can also destroy an organization too, but come to find out it wasn't passion lacking, out of three there was one that was a negative cancer who had joined forces with a PRN (as needed) employee and together they were trying to spread their negative infection by trying to erode the other two. The worst of the low performers (the negative duo) seemed to focus on frivolous stuff, first they couldn't even take care of my equipment and they wanted a new bed cover, guess what? A bed cover is not a "show-stopper," in as far as I was concerned I told them; the day you start worrying about the numbers I will get them whatever bed cover their heart desires and in any color!

In as far as I was concerned I wasn't bending backwards and spending corporate dollars for under-performers frivolous requests, other teams didn't have bed covers, learn how to do your job and maybe we can talk. The comical part of this is, I have two top-tier (Ace) performers, they come to work, they do their job, they help out where help is needed, they don't talk about anyone and they go home, those two never ask me for frivolous stuff, they don't complain, they don't have any forces of negative energy, they are self-starters and they are Critical thinkers, when they do make requests the requests are valid because they pertain to business in terms of supplies that will stop business if we don't have them. Their future is bright but I cannot leave this here without bragging on them, these two ladies are both mothers of three, they are Millennials! Whereas the other low performers are between the ages of 31 and 39, that's the one Millennial out of every Millennial that gives us a bad reputation.

Can you see what a difference these scenarios make? That my friends, is a critical thinking moment that Corporate America targets, they want those people that move forward in a positive manner, that type of attitude will carry you further than some that have been in your department for years! It's not the manager's job to think for you, every person has their own brain, I used to always make mention that I didn't get paid to think for people because if I did, I would have a whole different job title.

The single best advice I give college students about critical thinking is this: try and get a part time job if you can while you are in college, even a job that you work for one day out of the week, as being engaged in some type of job can benefit you in the long run and strengthen your critical thinking skills, truth be told, you can read all day long and all year long on "critical thinking" but unless you physically exercise critical thinking, then you won't get it, may I also mention that it's also great to see some type of work experience on a resume.

There is just something that won't come from the textbook when it comes to critical thinking. I have had employees literally complain about a room's temperature and yet the thermostat is perched on the wall within view. I held a meeting where I had to tell grown adults to shut the door that leads to the outside especially in the winter and summer.

I have had an employee tell me that they didn't have gas for the next day, so they didn't know how they were going to come to work. This is in real life y'all, I cannot make it up even if I tried; managers are not your parents and or sibling or relative unless you are actually related but my point is that you are not at home and the manager's job is not to address all your personal needs because one, they don't pay us enough for that and two we have our own personal issues to be concerned about.

I have a lot of examples on this, but I believe you get the point, be intuitive, pay attention to your surroundings and above all... use common logic.

Initiation

Most people that have made it to top-level positions are self-starters, people who are not afraid to initiate anything that needs to be done in the name of getting it done, I would once again suggest for college students or students that are in a working age to get a part-time job, one day out of the week or for a couple of days, whatever your life schedule can handle.

On the job skills that are typically observed or embedded in one's mind is the skill of initiation, this type of skill can also be found in those that have played sports in teams as well, managers and leadership admire and can readily recognize employees who have an initiation. This means that the individual is solution oriented and not problem focused.

The organization I worked for had set a standard for the candidates we hired for the Assistant Management position, at that time I was having a challenging time with the candidates that were being hired; most of them could not handle the position, with mounting frustration I needed to seriously get this position filled with someone that would be committed.

I sat back in deep thought and I remember seeing a girl who had worked with me for about two years at that time, she was a go getter, a self-starter, self-motivated and she took care of things on the team as though it was her job, she was basically doing things that an Assistant Manager would have been doing. She knew that I was having a hard time filling the Assistant Manager position, so she kicked into gear to help me without even asking me, she just took the initiation and went forward.

She saw that there was something that had to be done and she did it. I realized at the moment that my Assistant Manager had always been on the team, I contacted the Human Resources department expressing my desire to get this individual promoted, and I was of course hit with resistance because her position was not a position that fell in the category for cross-over into management.

I stood my ground, and I fought hard for her and guess what? They granted her access to the position. I remember it as though it was yesterday, I pulled her to the side and offered her the Assistant Management position with a pay increase, her eyes lit up, and she was excited then she became teary-eyed.

I knew then that was the right decision, she ended up working by my side for the next eight years or so. Understand that it's not just a great story of a promotion, she got a promotion because in my eyes she had already begun to carry the extra load that an Assistant Manager would have been doing.

She not only initiated but she never once asked me if she could do it; rather she noticed that supplies needed to be inventoried and that supplies needed to be ordered and that things needed organization so she just did what she saw needed to be done and therefore it was not hard for me to get her the promotion because she had already showed me the type of employee she was.

The problem with some employees is they like to talk a good game, they want the raise and or promotion but they don't want to work for it, understand that your work productivity and ethic is evident to whomever is watching; whether it's your manager or the owner of the company, no hard work goes unnoticed, promotions and raises might not come in the moment that you want but understand that for each person that is promoted ahead of you and for each person that is given a raise before you that means life is buying you time to keep sharpening your skills because maybe your promotion might be the position of CEO, so continue to work hard and diligently despite who is getting promoted or raises.

Even though her position did not cross-over to management, I fought tooth-and-nail for her because I knew her qualities, just like I fought tooth-and-nail for her, someone will and can possibly do that for you if you don't give up on yourself, trust me, you are being noticed or watched, over the years I have had employees try to tear down each other's performance to me as though I did not have eyes of my own, most times I came to notice that the employees that dug out the other employees performance are usually the ones that underperform, supervisors and managers typically notice every employee and know exactly who their strongest and weakest players are.

Your success or rate of rising today is a direct reflection of your performance in that organization, do not put a caption on what you can and cannot get promoted to. If you work hard and put in your sweat investment and show that you are positive, accountable and that you have the ability to take the initiation and are dependable, someone in leadership will notice you and if they don't notice you, your next level platform will. Remember life is a journey, you might just be that organization's next CEO in training, you just never know.

Self-sufficiency

Self-sufficiency is directly related to the process of initiation, understand that when you come into the world, your parents job for the most part is to help you adapt to society, they teach you the basics from an early age, they even teach you how to walk, talk and some parents will instill manners within your upbringing because they know that one day you will be on your own whether it's in college or living by yourself.

Most parents want their kids to be independent by the time they have to live by themselves. Every single time I train new hires, I like to equip them with everything they will need for their journey into their position, my goal is to leave no stones unturned during and after training and just like your parents, there comes a time when people will work with you to get you trained and situated for your position. After this has been done, the trainers or corporate expectations are that you will be able to function independently with self-sufficiency.

When you are going through your training process, make sure you understand what's going on and if not, feel free to ask as many questions as you want, leaders like to know that the employee they hired and trained is progressing within themselves, a year cannot go by and you are still asking basic questions that you should know or which you ought to have taken notes about.

One thing I learned about Corporate America is the simple fact that things don't fall on your laps, you are going to find yourself doing your own research at one point and time or familiarizing yourself with the company, it tickles me when an employee has been with the company for over six months and I say something to them and they say; "no one ever told me that."

Chances are that the employee is right but in a world where most corporations are pro-digital, then it is highly likely that all the information you need is found somewhere in a portal that you have access to so if you ever did something and were questioned by top-level leadership and your response was "no one ever told you," great chances are if there is a mistake that is rewarded by a consequence, they will still implement that consequence (write-up).

They would do that because it is your job to know what is expected of you, most corporations are lightening up their training programs so that they can be cost effective which means most times you are being trained to get into the position and after that you are on your own, for years I have always guided my new hires to the portal on the first day they started their training; mind you this is information that the Human Resources Department also gives them but I'd like the people to know.

It's not my responsibility to tell new hires all about the company's policies and all about the company. However, I always emphasize that you figure out where the handbook is, and you familiarize yourself with your company's policies. I cannot tell you how many people are ignorant about how to handle situations because they did not familiarize themselves with the company's policies and "I didn't know and or someone never told me" is not excuse enough to hold a person from being fired or getting documented because Corporate America doesn't have time for ignorance. Knowledge is always free-people! You just have to go digging for it, as a manager, I take no joy in issuing out disciplinary actions (as stated before), but I can write an entire book that will describe employees' ignorance that led to their termination. One quick example was a young lady we hired out of college, I emphasized as I do to everyone, I insisted for her to familiarize herself with the handbook, the handbook is the operating system of our company, needless to say, she never did and after she used up all her actions on tardiness; we had to part ways, had she read the handbook she would have understood that tardiness had a zero tolerance.

Understanding your organization's policies doesn't necessarily mean you will know more than the CEO, but it will place you in a confident zone. You will be able to perform your job with thorough knowledge of what the company expects of you and you have the great advantage of being able to grow into a self-sufficient employee, an employee that functions in self-sufficiency is one less person the manager has to worry about, employees that are self-sufficient typically get recognized more than the others that are not, because most managers will know that they can count on that employee to independently get their job done.

Remember that it's not your trainer's job to make you understand what the entire company policies are; rather it's your job to familiarize yourself with your organization's policies, understand that your job after training is to progress and not regress. Understand also that if you want to climb the rungs of Corporate America, self-sufficiency is of key importance.

Dress Code/Image

I have thoroughly highlighted the importance of understanding what your employer handbook expects of you as an employee, most handbooks will also have a dress code, know that every profession is different. Most of Corporate America is still at a business casual level unless specified. Therefore, unless you are working for Mark Zuckerberg, if you aspire growth within your position make it a point to dress the part, you do not have to start dressing like a CEO when you get the promotion. You can start now with your current position. Most times when I address dress code in my writing, I like to tread lightly because I do understand that not everyone works at the same place.

Next, I always have one rule of thumb which is: do not be in denial of your body shape. I understand that body image is a tough one, but you only do yourself a great service if you are genuinely honest with yourself. For instance, I know that I have a big chest, short thick thighs, and my grandma's butt plus child baring hips for days so, mermaid shaped skirts and or pencil skirts in which I love will not be so appropriate for me in a workplace.

Knowing that makes me understand in my profession that I need to buy slightly loose tops and baggy pants. My industry unfortunately doesn't have room for us to look sexy however we can look presentable. Understand both your body shape, and your clothing style, I had a new employee wear leggings with her uniform top (leggings are not a part of the uniform), I was utterly confused, who and where did she see that? She worked up a verbal warning courtesy of her own actions. Clearly she had not immersed herself in the employee handbook but at the same time, she had not seen anyone of the team members wear black leggings, it's really easy; "when in Rome do as the Romans," with a caution of course because as much as you can observe the dress code of those around, it doesn't mean you ought to ignorantly wear what is wrong. If a certain dress code is not permissible at your workplace, then please do not apply "when in Rome do as the Romans" at that point, instead apply "I have much more sense than that because I read the employee handbook."

    Speaking of "when in Rome do as the Romans," mind you each hired employee knows and understands the dress code because the Human Resources emphasizes the point and I always go over it with the newly hired candidate on their first day of work. I had a girl come to work in some Timberland boots. Shoe wear is white sneakers or crocs, it just blows my mind away when people do whatever they want, it never makes any logic to me because in that moment, I am being made into the uniform police who had to tell her what shoes to wear even though she knew that whole information because before the boots she was wearing white sneakers. All I say is do not be difficult, unless if it's your parents' company, then you would likely get away with it, as long as your parents do not own that company, I suggest you adhere to the dress codes in place. It would be unfair for me to leave this section without addressing the elephant in some people's rooms.

One thing I dread doing and I am pretty sure other managers and or leaders despise this one too so let's just dive into it, body hygiene once again it all depends on the profession that one is in but it's fair to say all professions deserve a fresh smelling person at work; I am just saying! It is not your manager's job to tell you that you have hygiene issues, I am not making fun of those that have clinical issues in this department, if you know you have clinical issues with body odor, understand that they make extra strength formulas for people to take advantage of, depending on your profession find out if you can wear cologne and or perfume.

A couple of years ago I had to make an intervention, this young lady's religion did not allow her to wear any deodorant or perfumes which I understood, but her body odor was getting a little too much, I was having her peers complaining to me and what came first was the patients' satisfaction. I had to talk to her which was not easy, I have friends of the same religion as hers, but they use natural oils and I never smelled any body odor from them, so I had to remind her of that particular example as well. I don't think it is fair to put anyone in the predicament to tell you about your body, if you know you take a shower every morning and powder up or deodorize, then do so, to keep yourself as well as other people safe.

    I am not going to spend a lot of time on this subject because we are all grownups, my grandmother always told me something that is very true, she always said if you can smell yourself then other people can smell you (verbatim in her words) and its true, I have experienced this after working up a sweat in the gym, I know my body and my pores. I am not the type that can take a shower at night and then just wake up and go to work, nope, this body doesn't play that. Even if I take a shower at night, I have to take another one in the morning because I tend to get extremely hot at night. I mention this because I know old habits are bad to kill off, perhaps since elementary school days you've been taking showers at night and just heading out in the morning and perhaps this is not going to work as effectively as it did when you were in elementary before puberty (I am just saying), Okay! That concludes hygiene, body image, etc.

Professionalism

Professionalism is contingent on the industry you choose to work even though I feel that every service provider should carry this ethic. We have mounting evidence of professionalism dying, it wasn't too long ago when a major airline dragged a paying customer out of the airplane (what happened to the customer is always right?) Understand that professionalism and customer service go hand in hand like Siamese twins at the hips.

America is driven by a stimulus of paying customers whether you are an engineer making software, you'd hope that the customer would buy that software and the customer is satisfied with the service provided, to the chef in a restaurant, Corporate America is all about numbers, whether you are in sales or the physical manufacturing portion of business, the nature of a business is that businesses are number driven for revenue and because of this; most businesses are customer or referral businesses, meaning that a little schmoozing and professionalism goes a long way especially now, in the era of online reviews.

Do you want to make it ahead? Professionalism will get you there! Most people (business people) will remember a person for their professionalism, and most business people will remember a rude person as well, no one is going to invest their money in a company where they don't feel valued and appreciated.

Professionalism is not just for your paying customers but also for the work-force, when you are at work you are not at home, most work-places have all kinds of employees from diverse backgrounds and ages. With that being said, don't come to work and act like you are at home, hollering all across the floor, being obnoxious or loud and so on. Pay attention to your environment, if you are working for a high-profile or a well-to-do attorney's office, the last thing you want to do is bring your home tendencies to work, your co-workers are not your sisters, brothers, mother and or father so they are not expected to treat you as such.

Keep all your weird home tendencies for home. We had a girl that thought since we were all cool with her, she could just use peoples personal supplies without asking, she had a rude awakening because I was one of those people that did not like people to touch my personal supplies (I mean I came prepared and my name is not OfficeMax), it kind of reminded me of the kid in school that never had any pens, papers and or textbooks but was always quick to mooch around the class for supplies.

I have always been the biggest advocate for students working in a customer-based industry, whether you are in college or high school. I am not insinuating working full-time, even part-time or as needed will help, working half a day on a Saturday can help an individual understand customer service, which helps with professionalism and skills for the work-force.

My first job was at 16 years old, I worked in a fine dining restaurant and because of the nature of the restaurant (fine dining that catered to a lot of "elites") I had to learn to be friendly, smile, make eye contact and actually engage in conversation. Before then I was a typical shy 16-year-old that was terrified of people seriously, most people today will tell me that I am a "people-person." I don't think I would have that caption if I never started in a customer-based industry that broke me out of my shell.

It is always important to govern yourself accordingly. Professionalism is just not an ACT of being but a WAY of being in the workplace. Some people dress and physically look professional and yet their mannerisms and being are really far from being professional. Please understand once again I am not insinuating that people shouldn't be themselves, rather I am stating that you should understand your environment and know how to present yourself according to that environment. Imagine if someone was just made junior partner with an established law firm and they have to represent you and in your first court appearance they are disrespecting the judge? That's totally unacceptable.

#The Millennial and The Work Place *Memory Bengesa*

Work Ethic

Some of you that have followed my YouTube channel or read some of my other books would find this next story a little familiar. My late *Gogo* (grandmother) once told me of a story when I was about 11 or 12 years old, that story stuck with me all these years and I thank my *Gogo* for her wisdom and our passing time in the smoky non-air-circulating hut back in the village in Zimbabwe.

Boy! I miss my *Gogo*. Picture this; nightfall befalls and we are literally out in the middle of nowhere, away from civilization as I like to say. The safest place to be when night time came was on the inside of the hut that my *Gogo* used as a kitchen, dining room, living room. Nonetheless; after dinner, she would entertain us by imparting words of wisdom by telling us traditional folklore stories. I can still feel the stinging of my eyes as the smoke from the fire filled the hut, the excitement in *Gogo's* voice was what always made story time epic. She said there was once a wealthy man in all the land who was well known for his riches, one day the man visited a small town and asked for a builder to build a home, the people gathered all the builders they knew except for one who was a crook. When the wealthy man started to address the group of builders, somehow this crook made his way into the gathering, at the sound of the wealthy man's plea for a builder the crook immediately threw his hand up and stated that he would build the home. The crowds grew loud as they jeered this crook, and finally, the wealthy man raised his hand to silence the roaring crowd. He wanted to hear this crook, so he asked him what he had said, the crook walked towards the wealthy man and stated he would be the guy for the job, the wealthy man paused, looked around and shook his head in consent, fine! He said. I want you to build the largest and most beautiful home you have ever built in your life.

The crowd went hysterical, some tried to warn the wealthy man, but he wasn't having it, he stated that he had found his guy and he trusted he was going to do a phenomenal job. With that, the wealthy man left the town. Months later he decided to pay the project a visit, unbeknownst to the wealthy man he was taken aback by the finished product, as he walked onto the property, the crook came to meet him, and the crook was excited to get paid.

He asked the wealthy man if he liked what he was seeing, the wealthy man shook his head in consent, he was still baffled at how fast the house had been built but the house looked extremely beautiful on the outside, the crook reached his hand out to give the wealthy man the key to the house, the wealthy man received the keys and clenched on to them, he stated to the crook, I don't know how you did it but you did it! Fantastic job! The builder was excited but seemingly wanted to get paid fast.

The wealthy man reached back out towards the builder and handed him the key, the builder was confused, the wealthy man put his hand on his shoulder and told him, this is a home for you and your family. I heard that your old house caught on fire, so I purposely came out with the intent to bless you with a living space for you and your family. I wanted it to be the best, biggest and most beautiful house you have ever built because everyone in life deserves a second chance. The builder was very reluctant to receive the keys, his face was as though he had seen a ghost, all he could utter was thank you and was frozen in place, but the wealthy man suspected it would take the builder a while to gather himself as he might have still been in shock by his generosity.

Once the wealthy man left the builder fell to his knees and cried like he had never cried before and no! It wasn't because of the man's generosity, he bawled like a little baby because he knew that the work he had done on the home was shady, he hadn't taken any time out to build a solid foundation, he just laid brick after brick ensuring the outside would look good enough and he would just get paid because that's what he was used to doing and that's why he was considered a crook. He also knew that he couldn't move his family into that house even if he tried because he knew the house would tumble down at any moment.

#The Millennial and The Work Place *Memory Bengesa*

So, in case you haven't figured it out, my *Gogo* hinted to me the importance of doing something to the very best no matter what it was and or who it was for. She told me this story as a reminder of what can happen in real life if we take the time to take full ownership of our job descriptions and give it a hundred percent. I do understand the moral to the story and being in leadership for so many years I can attest to the rewards of those that have ran businesses as though they were their own business and today they are CEO's or top executives.

I can also tell you lots of stories of those employees that came in and had the "I-just-work-here" attitude, those employees for the most part found themselves in the same positions and found themselves mumbling and grumbling over other people's promotions but it wasn't the other people's fault that they came in with a work ethic of addition to the company, if you desire top-level success, make sure you do everything with passion and zeal as though your name is on the marquee or outside the building. Remember: practice makes perfect, so let everything your hands touch be filled with a spirit of excellence, passion and zeal and knowing that at the end of the day, you have put in your best effort and you've done the best that you could possibly do.

Networking

In this section, I am going to write about *Networking* in two aspects. First, I want to write about you and social media. Understanding that online social media is now an easily accessible modern day communicative platform, social media is growing rampant especially with our generation and with that I also want to caution you because too much of everything is never good.

Recently our employer has embarked on the band-wagon of social-media-profile potential candidate perusing, meaning that most of you have already heard this part so please understand that it is actually true, if you desire top-level or growth within your professional career, it is important to once again govern yourself accordingly meaning making sure your personal Facebook profile is private, or other social media outlets are private.

If there is anything on there that your co-workers would never believe you do, e.g. a junior high school or High school teacher who is in pursuit of becoming a principal and yet on your

Facebook you are in a scene with people popping Molly and doing all kinds of things that your employer should not see!

You will not believe how many times this has hindered potential candidates, I know most of you are thinking; who in the world doesn't use a privacy setting for their Facebook and other social media-right? Well! This also goes as far as the "professional" platforms (yup!)

True story: we had a candidate that seemed promising but corporate did further digging and found him on the big "professional" site and he had all his tattoos showing and big-ol ear gauges so guess what? They shut that down before he even started. I would have thought that people would understand that it was a "professional" platform but I guess he did not get the MEMO, once again depending on where and what your work culture is it might be acceptable. Our culture at that moment was not the tattoo and gauge wearing environment, so please do your best to be aware of your involvement and activity on certain social media platforms. Secondly, I want to talk about the advantage of social media for getting ahead. Back in the day when I started my career I was quite the shy type (believe it or not) and it did not help that I was an introvert, also back in the day before the advancements of social media platforms for professional networking, I literally had to go to these networking events which I dreaded (I am such an introvert).

It made me feel uncomfortable and uneasy talking to people I had never met a day in my life, thank goodness those days are gone. I had to do that as a Vice President of a 501 c3 non-for-profit that I volunteered for, I needed connections and resources to help this international organization so hence, I had to go and network face-to-face.

Nowadays you have the power of the "Google tool" at your disposal to guide you on different networking groups online and even in person. My advice is at least once in your lifetime get the chance to network with those that are out of your company's reach, it helps you grow within your position and over time you will build great relationships with other people that can eventually help you with the next steps of your career. Remember it all starts with a simple "hello," over the years I have taught myself to become accustomed to the whole networking culture; not fully adjusted but accustomed to the art of networking, if I can do it you can as well. You must remember that most people want to make it to the top and sometimes it's not what you know or how you know, but it's really who you know.

Mentors

Once I gained my little "networking" muscle, I managed to muster up enough confidence to ask some of the networking contacts to be my mentors. There was a point and time in my life where I felt like okay, I need a coach or mentor; that person that has walked in these shoes to be my soundboard and or fountain of wisdom. My siblings are amazing counselors, they are like most siblings who are proud of their sister and sometimes I feel like they want to say all the right things but most times, I felt as though they were my number one fans and what I wanted was someone or people that would really challenge me to think because I wanted to grow more than where I was, leadership is very tricky because you get used to creating and implementing so-much-so that you don't really have anyone at the moment to challenge you.

Employees are not going to do it in fear of insubordination and or because they might be afraid to ask their boss why we have to do this-that-and-the-other. So, yes! Naturally, I am human too, and I wanted that guidance, for the longest time I thought mentors where people that would just cross your path and tell you that they want to mentor you. Small wonder why I didn't have a mentor for a long time. I got a harsh reality, and one day I grew tired of waiting, and I decided to reach out to my boss, he was the first person I could think of in terms of mentorship, I asked him and he gladly accepted, that was a relief and I got the confidence I needed to ask the rest of the people that I wanted to ask.

I realized that all I had to do was just ask. In the worst case a person may say no but at least you would have asked. I am glad I asked my boss as a first option, because of him I managed to really grow into my leadership role. He was very knowledgeable; patient and he challenged my thinking to grow and to think more and more like a top-level leader. Above all, he believed in me so-much-so that it reflected in my performance.

It's not every day that a boss can be a mentor but its every day that you can find an opportunity to get a mentor, trust me. There is no room to act like you are the only one that knows it all at the top, at the top you will have advisors, counselors and a whole caucus of different ideologies that you will have to respect because a great organization is not run off one person's might.

I hate to burst your bubble, but remarkable success involves a team of people, when was the last time you ever heard of a movie winning an Academy Award from one person? Even a song, face it! It takes the singer sometimes the lyricist, and then you need the producers etc. The same thing with a movie, it needs all the people that are behind the scenes to make it a success. Teamwork really is such an important thing!

Get-Ahead and Stay-Ahead

I have given you substantial advice from my individual experiences in Corporate America so that you can climb the rungs of the corporate ladder, in this last portion; I want to highlight some realities. I believe that you really should be honest with yourself first for all other things to manifest in your life.

Why do you want to climb the ladder? What is your intention? Where is your heart on this matter? Years ago, when I started working, I had unrealistic goals for the credentials I wanted to obtain so that I could climb the corporate ladder faster, after failed goals and goals that were never accomplished I became very frustrated, amid being frustrated I started to become confused on what I really wanted to do and be in terms of career progression.

I started to apply to different universities to advance my career, application after application I was failing, something was not right, after all who gets this much difficulties in America for trying to attend a university? But the truth was that was not where my heart was, I was making hasty decisions because I thought it would help me move up in Corporate America, I wanted to advance my education to advance my career but at this point and time, I didn't want to be in debt because my parents and I had just paid off the balance for my earlier education and I kind of wanted to enjoy my career pay. I couldn't get financial help because I made too much money, they wanted me to take out school loans and I didn't want to be in debt because at that time I was living in my brand new custom-built dream home, so I didn't want to incur another loan, the truth of the matter was that this was not my destiny at that time. Now that I evaluate that episode in my life, I can truly say so because if it were something that my heart truly desired or which destiny had in store for me.

I am pretty sure I would have moved mountains and wouldn't have thought twice about being in debt. Some years went by and as I continued to do some soul searching, I managed to attain my first promotion which got me excited, but I still did not feel like that was it, I endeavored to continue to work hard in hopes of a continual Corporate America ladder climb. I want to keep it one hundred percent real with you (as we Millennials say! Keeping it 100), at the start of this section I highlighted the need to know of one's true intentions through a thorough heart search.

Corporate America is a for-profit organization, one that sometimes seeks to get the cream of the crop employees and one that also comes with all kinds of politics. I don't have the magic recipe for you to get to that CEO position, however I have given you some of the essential tools and with that, it's also my responsibility to tell you that Corporate America is not so "cookie-cutter," I wish I could tell you, work hard, play hard, show up on time and leave late and you will get that promotion—no, that's not how it goes for some. I will keep saying evaluate your heart and your soul's truth for the real reason you desire to climb the ladder.

It didn't take me long to know that I had to do some soul-searching, I thought I was doing everything I needed to do to get ahead, I kept my numbers up and ran a solid ship and year after year, my colleagues were getting "bigger" promotions. The hardest thing for me at that time was watching people come in, get hired without the experience and or credentials and get significant promotions than myself. Honestly my feelings were hurt because I knew what type of employee I was (oh—yes! There is lots of politics in Corporate America, but never be discouraged).

I became so upset that I was willing to jeopardize my position because I had now become upset with "Corporate America." How dare they pass me up, I had been working for them so many years and I busted my butt all the way! I went above and beyond, and I ran a solid ship...I...I...I oh! It became an "I" fest in my life so much so that I started looking for other employment opportunities that would find me valuable.

Truth be told, if you are frustrated with where you are and want to leave, the chances are you will be frustrated with where you go, never leave one unresolved frustrating situation for another because you stand a chance of bringing that toxic energy to the new environment, I went on multiple interviews (top-tier) positions, I mean five or six stage interviews. Finally, someone knew my value or so I thought, interview after interview I didn't feel internally satisfied, the offers were good, some wanted to pursue me and others didn't and it just felt good at the moment knowing that people admired my work and wanted me as a part of their organization. My serial interview campaign to validate my worth was unsatisfying, yet I did it.

  I was able to prove the fact that I could be a "top-tier" leader but still, deep down inside my soul, I was not fulfilled. I sat there and looked at the offers and realized that I would be leaving one set of politics to go into another and I had to ask myself if that was what I truly wanted or if I just wanted the validation. What am I saying? I apologize, but I am being repetitious for a reason.

  You have to conduct a deep soul search on your ambitions and aspirations; I realized that I wanted that "ultimate" promotion because I believed that's what should've happened next when in actuality, that wasn't it. See, my entire life was surrounded by a mentality of: you go to school, you land the job, then you climb the ladder, you have made it. That was my thought of the epitome of success in America until I wasn't climbing the rungs of the Corporate Ladder anymore. I realized my intentions were not soulfully placed, that was not what my heart wanted, but that was what my mind wanted as a "show-and-tell" of success.

When I realized this; I had another epiphany, I didn't want a "show-of-success" life if it meant gutting and cutting the next man to get into a higher position. I wanted peace of mind and I also wanted to live a fulfilled life. At this point, I had been writing for years, recreationally and managed to publish one book. I had an epiphany; *"why am I waiting on someone else to give me a promotion?"* OMG! I finally got it! What I thought of success all these years wasn't it.

Success is what you do and doing it well satisfies you, and you have come to full terms of embracing it and it makes you happy and it makes you want to love and live a life. With that realization, I got to the point where I realized that all these years I had been basking in my closeted self-gratifying hobby (writing) that would actually benefit others. I chose to give myself a promotion. I love the art of speaking so I got a speaking coach, I had been writing and lived and breathed writing, so I got a writing mentor. When I started focusing on who I really was, my internal heart compass made a switch, I was satisfied, I was fulfilled.

Sure, more and more unqualified people that had been there fewer years than me continued to get promotions but this time around; it didn't bother me anymore because I had found me! I had truly found myself, what moved me and made me. What am I saying? I thought you were supposed to help us get ahead? hear me out, there are some of you that are designed by the destiny of our creator to climb the rungs of Corporate America and then there are some of you out there that are created to be like the next Bill Gates, defy the odds, take a different path and produce your own product that will move you to your own fulfillment, who am I to give you all the tools to get ahead in Corporate America and neglect those that are not destined to being in Corporate America for the rest of their lives? I told you it was getting really real.

However, before you and I get to our intended destiny, we do have the current platform that we work in, whether your destiny is a promotion within your workplace or your own company; understand that you still need the building blocks of understanding how to work for someone else so that the best of your abilities can shine through because true masters are those that have been doing it for a while, so no! I did not waste your time giving you all the "get-ahead" advice, matter-of-fact all the "get-ahead" advice works for you right now and when you embark on your destiny. I don't want to create a false hope like I had; I don't want you to believe that life consists of fair acknowledgements that lead to rewards such as promotions and bigger bonuses.

The truth is, some of you will be treated unfairly even if you are a hard worker but don't let that ruin your character (remember *Gogo's* story), some of you will be passed up on bonuses or promotions even though you know you deserve it. This is not a reflection on you and or your character; sometimes it's the politics of Corporate America that gets in the way, the who-you-know-antics, some of you will be in the same position for years and to you I say work your platform like no other and dig into your heart, find out what is life preparing you for? I would be lying if I said that Corporate America is the fairest platform on the earth.

Please understand that you are all unique, with different gifts and talents and definitely different goals and ambitions, tap into your heart. What do you want out of life? Who are you? What defines you? Who are you without that career? I am a strong believer that everything happens for a reason, yes! Even the unexplainable and maybe that's got something to do with my faith but in all sincerity, you are where you are today because that is the experience or platform you need to get to wherever your heart wants you to get to in life, even if you are a nurse that wants to pursue a whole different industry, your patience in that industry will carry over to your next paradigm.

This book consists of habits and advice that will help you get ahead at your current workplace and your intended destiny, even if you are the small percent of people that knows that you are not going to retire from your organization because you will own your own company at the end of the day, I say that you use this current platform as a way to get-ahead, you get to see and observe how you want to run your organization, also always maintain a great work ethic, treat everything you do with excellence because remember my *Gogo's* story, one day you too might own a company and or could have that "Ultimate" promotion and you can only get to the top if you value excellence, hard work, commitment, dedication and you are able to identify your soul's intent.

At the end of the day, go out there! Show up! Show off! And work your hardest!

Acknowledgements

When I look at my life's journey I notice people that God strategically placed in my path so that I too can get ahead and stay ahead, to these men and women; I appreciate you and thank you for giving me a chance and for believing in me and my potential, the list is longer and for those I have been unable to mention I appreciate you, I am grateful and indebted.

- Joe M
- Mrs. M
- My siblings
- Christy M
- Dr. George C
- Shanna P
- Reshef
- K.C.M

Join the discussion on social media! Don't forget to Hashtag!

www.MemoryBengesa.com

MemoryBengesa@Twitter.com

MemoryBengesa@instagram.com

MemoryBengesa@YouTube

www.facebook.com/bookmemorybengesa

#TheMillennial&TheWorkPlace

#TMATWP

www.ingramcontent.com/pod-product-compliance
Lightning Source LLC
LaVergne TN
LVHW011215080426
835508LV00007B/792